LONDON MIDLAND

STEAM ON SHED

INDUSTRIAL STEAM

...NER STEAM

ELECTRIC...

SOUTH... WORKS ... STEAM

BR S... BRITA...

SOUTHERN ... IN ACTION

...EL ...WER

...ND THE WORLD

...OTTISH

BORDERS STEAM

MAIN LINE STEAM

LIGHT RAILWAYS

standard gauge and narrow gauge

OF BRITAIN

BRIGHTON

india

STEAM IN india

ARTICULATED LOCOMOTIVES OF THE WORLD

SCOTTISH RAILWAYS in the heyday of steam

...MIDLANDS

2

... Boyd

THE WELSH NARROW GAUGE

STEAM ...RIGHT

2 ROUND THE WORLD

SUPERPOWER STEAM

BRITISH TRAMS

GREAT WESTERN STEAM THROUGH THE YEARS

SCOTTISH

WESTERNS

the later years of

BRANCH LINE STEAM

BR CLASS 5

THE MIDLAND RAILWAY

LMSR LOCOMOTIVES

GREAT WESTERN

BR STANDARD
BRITANNIA PACIFICS

a study of British Railways Standard Class 7P express passenger locomotive

edited by G. Weekes

D. BRADFORD BARTON LTD

Frontispiece: BR Standard Class 7P 'Britannia' Pacific No. 70004 *William Shakespeare* at Stewarts Lane shed, 2 April 1955, with 'Golden Arrow' headboard, flags and emblem. This locomotive, turned out from Crewe works on 29 March 1951, was specially finished for display at the Festival of Britain exhibition in London that year. No. 70004 received special treatment in the paintshop, albeit in Standard BR livery, whilst all exposed pipework, motion, etc., was burnished or chromium-plated. Brought down 'dead, own wheels' from the works to Willesden depot, No. 70004 was on display at the South Bank site of the Festival beside the Thames from 4 May to 30 September and started work on the 'Golden Arrow' service to and from Dover on 11 October, based on Stewarts Lane shed in South London.   [Brian Morrison]

© copyright D. Bradford Barton Ltd 1975 ☐ ISBN 0 85153 195 4 ☐ Set in Monotype Bembo and printed by offset litho by H. E. Warne Ltd, of London and St. Austell, for the publishers D. Bradford Barton Ltd, of Trethellan House, Truro, Cornwall.

THE last class of express passenger locomotive built in Britain as well as the last to remain in service were the 7P Pacifics, known as the 'Britannias', in the standard series of designs produced by British Railways consequent upon nationalisation in 1948. In essence, the 'brief' for the design team assembled by BR was to provide a fast mixed-traffic locomotive that would be suitable for use on all the Regions into which the nation's railway network had been divided. To wide route availability had to be added the need for relatively inexpensive capital cost and—no less important—inexpensive maintenance. This meant two cylinders and a design without frills. Rugged in the American style and as functional as a Continental machine, it also had to be acceptable to conservative English footplate and shed staff nurtured in a love of 'Royal Scots' or A3s, 'Castles' or 'West Countries'. No. 70000 *Britannia* was completed at Crewe by the end of 1950, and steamed on 2 January 1951. In appearance she showed obvious LMSR parentage, looking not unlike a smaller up-dated version of the 'Duchesses'. Leading dimensions were: 6′ 2″ coupled wheels, 250 lbs. boiler pressure, 20″ x 28″ cylinders, grate area 42 sq. ft., total evaporative heating surface 2,474 sq. ft. Plate frames, a wide firebox, roller bearings on coupled wheels, a big free-steaming taper boiler, a large and well-laid out cab, completed the picture. The relatively small BR1 class tender, with inset coal bunker, was the only major outward variation from LMSR design. Somewhat surprisingly, a single blastpipe was incorporated, the shallow chimney necessitating large deflector plates to obviate any problems from drifting smoke. With an axle load just exceeding 20 tons, route availability was a good as a 'Castle' or a rebuilt 'Royal Scot', and with a 58′ 3″ overall wheelbase, a 'Britannia' could just be accommodated on a 60′ turntable. It is interesting to study the class in terms of nominal performance with the other Class 7 designs with which they might fairly be compared. Tractive effort at 85 per cent nominal rating was 32,150 lbs.; that for a rebuilt 'Royal Scot' 33,150 lbs., and a 'Castle' 31,625 lbs. Locomotive weights available for adhesion for these three classes came out almost alike, with 60 tons 15 cwt., 61 tons and 59 tons respectively. And therein lay something of the answer to the surer starting capabilities of the 4-6-0s, where weight transference came back entirely on to the driving wheels and the harder the acceleration the more this was the case. Even though all-up weight of the 'Britannia' was 94 tons 4 cwt. (compared with 83 tons for a 'Scot' and only 80 for a 'Castle') the trailing truck—as with almost all Pacifics—made for a machine that needed careful handling to get away without slipping, particularly over the mass of point-work at main station exits.

The initial batch of 'Britannias' (Nos. 70000-70024), came out from Crewe during 1951, two for LM Region, eight for Western Region and fifteen—the first ones built—for Eastern Region. These latter were for service on the GE main line out of Liverpool Street, with the intention of accelerating the Ipswich and Norwich services. In this, the new Pacifics succeeded admirably, with the Stratford and Norwich crews taking to their charges extremely well. Elsewhere, on Western Region—as is now well-known—reaction to the 'Britannias' was less favourable. Diehard footplatemen reared in the long Churchward/Collett tradition could find little to praise in a Crewe-built smoke-deflectored Pacific with a left-hand driving position and an all-enclosed cab. The main complaint of senior drivers was that 'Britannias' were prone to slip—as indeed they were if a driver was used to the greater adhesion of a 4-6-0 and the greater sensitivity of a Swindon regulator. Dire tales were told of them slipping to a stand on the 1 in 100 up through Box Tunnel and of similar troubles coming out of the Severn Tunnel after being slowed or brought to a stand by p.w. checks in the dip. WR men were not used to Pacifics and some of this reputation of slipperiness could be traced to mishandling.

After all the WR locomotives had been concentrated at Cardiff, the Canton men grew to like them tolerably well. They were found to be as free-running as a 'Castle' and as fast, with a better boiler for steam output, yet lighter on consumption of coal. The three principal South Wales expresses worked by the shed became regular 'Britannia' turns. More widespread were complaints that the class were hard-riding, noisy and dirty. Although lateral riding was good, vibration in the cab made footplate work tiring, particularly for the fireman and no real cure for this rough riding at the back end was to be found. As one writer, versed in footplate affairs, put it—a 'Britannia' "should have had a silencer and springs". Other design modifications were needed (as detailed subsequently in this volume) and these were incorporated in the second batch of 20 (Nos. 70025-44) built 1952-53.

A further batch of ten was constructed in 1954, again all products of Crewe works, Nos. 70045-54. These were for LM Region, initially for Holyhead and Polmadie (Glasgow) and had the larger 9-ton capacity BR1D tenders. These were high-sided curved-in tenders rather similar to those of the LMS 'Duchess' class and gave a smoother airflow around the locomotive cab than was the case with the earlier tenders with inset sides. At speed these latter created a back draught of air swirling around the eaves of the cab roof which made the problem of dirt and airborne coal dust much worse. On this score, the cleaner 'office' for the crew with a conventional tender was vastly preferred to the advantage—only infrequently needed—of a good view of the road when backing down tender-first.

'Britannias' ranged far and wide during their period of service, being regularly seen at locations as far apart as Aberdeen and Bournemouth, Neyland and Norwich, Stranraer and Dover. At one time or another they were to be seen, for example, at every one of the main termini in London. Their range of operations widened even more noticeably towards the end of steam when they had been displaced by diesels from their usual express passenger turns.

The shortcomings of the class are mentioned elsewhere in this volume; for a more technical analysis the interested reader is referred to *BR Standard Steam Locomotives* (E. S. Cox) and the Profile publication on the 'Britannias' (Brian Reed). The most dramatic troubles were those afflicting the axles, soon after introduction, and the parting of the engine-tender drawbar on various of the class in the 1957-58 period.

To keep the matter of 'teething' troubles of the class in true perspective, comparison might usefully be made with the initial period of service of the Bulleid Pacifics on the Southern which for some months were relegated to freight duties only, as failures were so frequent. One should recall in this respect that the 'Britannias' were introduced at a period when the performance and character of new locomotives aroused widespread interest amongst a vastly increased number of steam enthusiasts; minor shortcomings were much more widely noted in the 1950s than had been the case in the 1930s. With pre-war standards of maintenance and footplate work, the full potential of the 'Britannias' as sound, reliable machines comparable with any other British Pacific would have been realised. In day-to-day service, the 'Britannias' were as reliable and hardworking as other comparable classes; the era in which they saw service was, literally, the twilight of steam when conditions were very far different from the pre-war standard of shed maintenance and footplate morale. Running costs and mileage between repairs compared favourably and it was no mere accident of fate that 'Britannias' were the last Pacifics to remain.

One minor point about the 'Britannias', from their wide distribution over the years, was that they probably carried a more varied selection of named train headboards than any other class of locomotive in Britain. To mention but a few these included 'The Golden Arrow' and the 'Bournemouth Belle'; various South Wales expresses including 'The Red Dragon' and the 'Capitals United Express'; 'The Cornishman' on occasion and 'The Pines Express' at least once, on the section north of the S. & D.; 'The Irishman', to and from Stranraer; 'The Thames-Clyde Express', 'The Palatine' and 'The Irish Mail'; 'The Master Cutler' and 'The Fenman'; and virtually all the numerous East Anglian expresses, ranging from 'The Hook Continental' to the little-known 'Easterling'.

Withdrawal of the 55 locomotives in the class began in mid-1965 with No. 70007 *Coeur de Lion* and No. 70043 *Lord Kitchener*, condemned in June and August respectively. Another ten were withdrawn in 1966 and the remainder in batches during 1967. Two have now been preserved, No. 70013 *Oliver Cromwell* at Bressingham Steam Museum and No. 70000 *Britannia*, namesake of the class. The latter is owned by a private society who rescued and have valiantly restored it following its disposal for scrap consequent upon the BR decision to preserve No. 70013 instead.

The 'Britannias' were undoubtedly a handsome and well-balanced design, that would stand aesthetic comparison with any other British design of Pacific locomotive. And in condemning the degree of functional ugliness, chiefly evident in the exposed piping and high-set running plate, one should remember this was a locomotive designed in 1950—and not 1930—when the needs for modest capital cost and ease of maintenance were very different. The 'Britannia' pedigreee obviously harked back to Crewe, the majority of the design team being ex-LMSR men.

Completed early in January 1951, No. 70000 ran trials between Crewe and Carlisle, after a period of running-in, and then re-emerged from the paintshop in standard BR green livery ready for the naming ceremony at Marylebone on 30 January. Shedded at Stratford, she entered service on 1 February, working services on the GE main line. The name *Britannia* had been carried by an LMS 'Jubilee', No. 45700, which was accordingly re-named *Amethyst* late in 1951 to avoid duplication. No. 70000 is now preserved at Bridgnorth, one of two of the class that survived the breaker's torch.

[Brian Morrison]

An up express from Clacton thunders through Marks Tey station behind No. 70002 *Geoffrey Chaucer*, 21 March 1959. The Class 40 diesel-electrics and their successors had begun to displace the 'Britannias' on the East Anglian services about this time and the Stratford allocation was moved out to join the others already at Norwich shed.   [M. Mensing]

No. 70001 *Lord Hurcomb* breasts the summit of the 1 in 100 climb of Brentwood bank in fine style with the down 'East Anglian' for Norwich, in June 1954. Above, No. 70013 *Oliver Cromwell*, on the same evening, with steam off for the run down the bank with 'The Norfolkman' from Yarmouth, due to arrive at Liverpool Street at 7.55 p.m.   [Brian Morrison]

After the first eight of the class had been allocated to Stratford until 1959, as already noted), the next six went to Norwich, including No. 70011 *Hotspur*, seen here ready to leave Platform 4 at Norwich on March 1958 on the .45 p.m. to Liverpool Street via Ipswich. The Britannias' established fine reputation on the ex-GE main line—a route by no means as easy as might be thought—and after being in service for a few years were regularly taking 12 coach loads of 400 tons or so on the Norwich expresses in under 120 minutes including the Ipswich stop.

[J. R. Besley]

No. 70005 *John Milton* passing through Woodbridge in Suffolk in August 1958 with the down 'Easterling'—the comparatively unknown named express that ran, in summer only, between Liverpool Street and Great Yarmouth.

[Malcolm Dunnett]

The introduction of the 'Britannias' was marked by troubles in their first summer of service; initially this was in the form of cylinder damage caused by unsatisfactory design in the shallow steam dome, which caused severe priming and permitted water to surge down to the cylinders under certain conditions. More serious was the second bout of trouble which affected No. 70004 *William Shakespeare*, which suffered a broken coupling rod whilst working the 'Golden Arrow' on 21 October. Other 'Britannias' too had been plagued by similar dangerous breakdowns, due to the coupled wheels shifting on their hollow axles, and throughout November all the 25 of the class were withdrawn from service for modification. No. 70004 (seen here outside Swindon works in 1960) was back in regular service on the Southern by 7 December and all the remainder by early 1952.   [R. J. Leonard]

After completion of the first 25 'Britannias' by September 1951, a further second batch of 20 (Nos. 70025-44) was put in hand. There were minor improvements to these, apart from the running gear modifications already shown to be necessary, principally to balancing in an endeavour to improve riding, to the cab-tender region to improve cab comfort, and to the tender drawbar (as detailed later). No. 70037 *Hereward the Wake*, delivered in December 1952 (photographed at Stratford on 7 July 1956), was one of seven in this batch that went to Eastern Region. Others went to the LM and Western Regions.   [Brian Morrison]

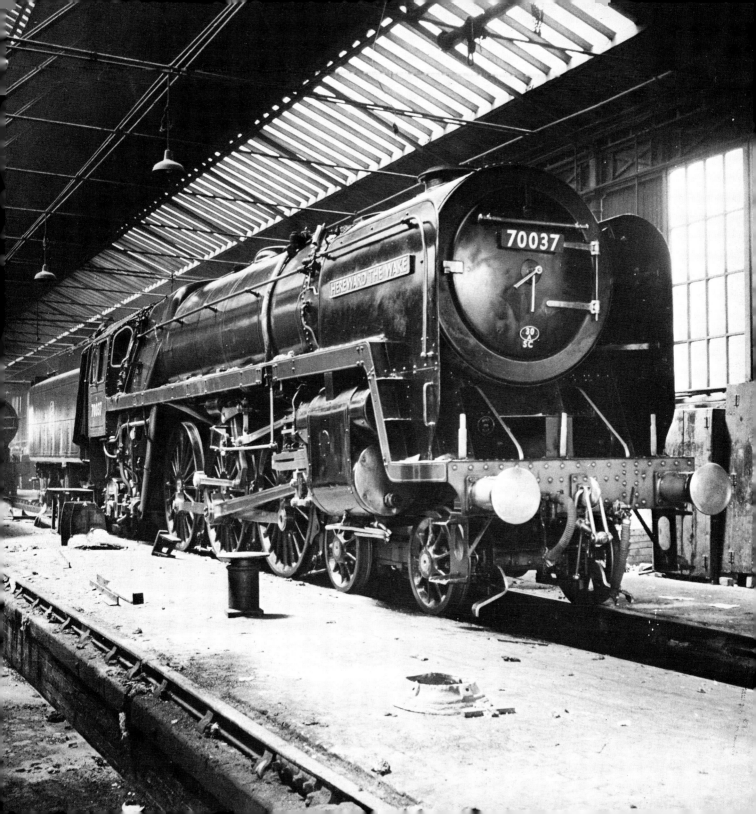

Eastern Region 'Britannias' at Kings Cross: right, No. 70041 *Sir John Moore* (built March 1953) on 13 October 1962 [W. L. Underhay]: below, No. 70039 *Sir Christopher Wren* waiting in the loco yard on 26 April 1961 and (opposite) departing later the same day with an express for the north.
[G. A. Richardson]

Eight of the first series of 'Britannias' went to Western Region in the summer of 1951, four to Old Oak Common, two to Laira and two to Newton Abbot. Reaction by ex-GW men was unfavourable, on several counts—compounded of the real and the imaginary, of which an active dislike of anything 'non-Swindon' was perhaps the most important. Drivers did not like 'slippery' Pacifics, more particularly those with left-hand drive and alien-looking smoke deflectors which impaired their view of the road; firemen did not like the novelty of a wide firebox; and neither liked the hard ride that every 'Britannia' undoubtedly gave its crew. However, the first five of the second batch (Nos. 70025-29) were allocated to Cardiff (Canton) and there by contrast they quickly won themselves an entirely satisfactory reputation. The opportunity was then taken by the authorities to transfer there by the end of 1956 all the earlier ones (Nos. 70017-24) as well, in exchange for 'Castles'. 'The Capitals United' and 'The Red Dragon' then became regular 'Britannia' turns, No. 70018 *Flying Dutchman* being seen above on the latter express at Paddington in August 1957. [A. R. Butcher]

A Canton 'Britannia', No. 70028 *Royal Star*, taking life easy with a north-bound Hereford-Shrewsbury local at All Stretton Halt, 10 June 1957—probably on a spell of secondary work following overhaul or heavy repair at Swindon. The WR-allocated 'Britannias' bore the names of old GWR locomotives   [M. Mensing]

The high regard of the Norwich men for their 'Britannias' was in complete contrast to that of the ultra-conservative WR crews and shed staff, and these locomotives gave sterling service in East Anglia until replaced by dieselisation there. No. 70040 *Clive of India* is waiting to leave the murky darkness of Liverpool Street with the 5.40 p.m. to Clacton on 9 September 1958 whilst, opposite, are two scenes at Ipswich. No. 70012 *John of Gaunt* is in sparkling condition in November 1957 shortly after a visit to works, and is about to leave with a train from Yarmouth (South Town), whilst No. 70008 *Black Prince* waits to leave with an evening train to Liverpool Street on 23 May 1958.

[J. R. Besley]

A pair of the first ER 'Britannias', No. 70009 *Alfred the Great* and No. 70014 *Iron Duke*, were loaned for a time to Southern Region to test driver reaction to the new class as well as to assess their capabilities in their hands. Here, the first of the two heads the down 'Bournemouth Belle' near Eastleigh on 11 September 1951. Later, in 1953, ten of the WR 'Britannias' were loaned to the Southern for a period, to replace the 'Merchant Navy' Pacifics which had been temporarily withdrawn.

[Brian Morrison]

During the relatively brief period that 'Britannias' appeared on Southern metals, No. 70014 *Iron Duke* heads a down relief Dover express past Bickley Junction in Kent, 11 August 1951.

[Brian Morrison]

No. 70014 continued in regular service on the 'Golden Arrow' during 1952-3 and became well liked by the Stewarts Lane men. Here she runs fast down Hildenborough bank on 23 May 1953 at the head of the ten-coach set of umber-and-cream Pullman cars.

[Brian Morrison]

No. 70014 *Iron Duke* at Stewarts Lane on 1 April 1958, ready to work the 'Golden Arrow'. The shed here had a well-deserved reputation for the standard of cleanliness and day-by-day maintenance lavished on their top link locomotives. *Iron Duke* was regarded as one of the best of the class.

[A. R. Butcher]

The driver's side of No. 70019 *Lightning*, one of the pair of much maligned 'Britannias' allocated to Newton Abbot shed, seen at Old Oak Common on 20 March 1955. Later this locomotive was based on Cardiff (Canton). Part of the WR crews' dislike of these Pacifics was due to their insensitive regulators—compared with the Swindon type—which they maintained prevented them from getting away 'clean'. Over and above this, the 'Britannias' were undoubtedly hard riding, particularly so compared to Pacifics with coil spring trailing trucks.   [Brian Morrison]

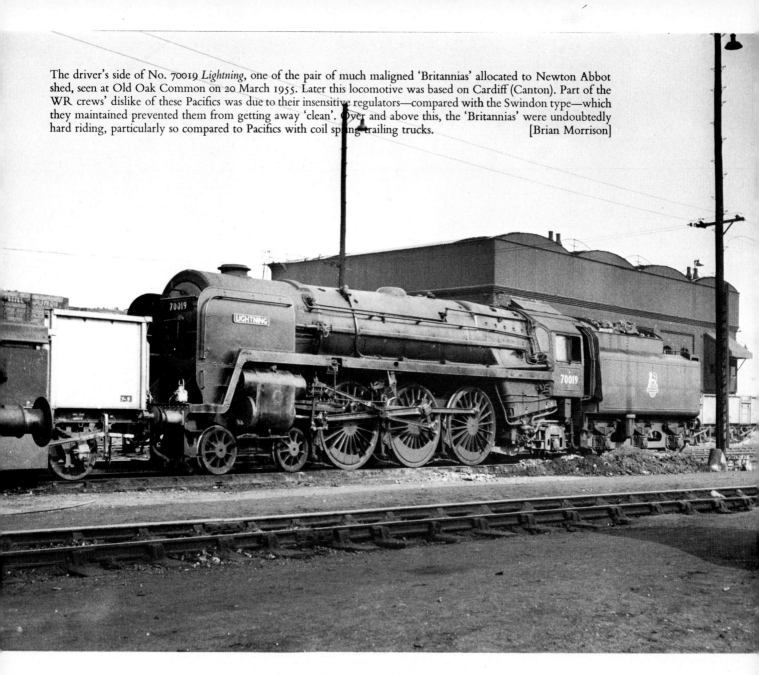

A close-up of the cylinder and bogie, etc., of No. 70022 *Tornado* (photographed at Crewe South, 15 January 1967). The Walschaerts valve gear with three-bar crosshead and slide, cylinders (20″ × 28″) and valves were of the same design dimensions as the 9F Standard 2-10-0s. Bogie and coupled wheel diameters were 3′ and 6′ 2″ respectively.   [N. E. Preedy]

The nearside
motion and
running gear of a
'Britannia' showing
the 6'2" diameter
drivers. This
example (No.
70013) has the
revised plain
rectangular-
section leading and
rear coupling rods,
in place of the
original fluted
type.

[N. E. Preedy]

The nearside
cylinder of No.
70026 *Polar Star*
with the front
cover off, exposing
the piston. These
latter were of cast
steel, with bronze
slipper; later a
lighter forged-
steel head was
substituted, butt-
welded to the
piston rod.
Cylinder cocks, as
in the 9F, were
steam operated.

[E. N. Kneale]

A view along the boiler barrel of No. 70053 *Moray Firth*, December 1965. Note the two Ross pop safety valves recessed in the boiler cladding and the low steam dome—not as squat in shape as the one originally specified on early 'Britannias' - and the single chimney. The class ran with the latter all their lives, double blastpipes and chimneys being considered at one stage but never fitted.

[D. M. Cox]

A near head-on view of No. 70012 with nameplates removed, as running in April 1967. Detail differences are visible from her appearance as built, notably the lack of handrails on the smoke deflectors, repositioned lamp brackets, and an extended step below the smoke-box door. No. 70012 was one of the class which experienced the alarming occurrence of the parting of the engine and tender when the drawbar broke, in 1957 near Ilford whilst working a down express. This happened to various of the 'Britannias' about this time and their drawgear was altered in design and strength on all the class to prevent its occurrence again.

[D. M. Cox]

'Britannias' and other LM Region locomotives on shed at Crewe North 1965. In the foreground is No. 70047 which was the only one of the 55 'Britannias' never to bear a name. No. 70049 *Solway Firth* was the last to be named, in the summer of 1960.

[J. R. Carter]

The chime whistle of 'Britannias' was mounted on the righthand front end of the boiler barrel and operated by Bowden cable running through the hand-rail. Condensation collecting in the supply steam pipe was responsible for a variety of notes in practice!

[J. R. Carter]

The lefthand nameplate of No. 70054 *Dornoch Firth*, last of the 'Britannias', built in September 1954. The 'Firths' (Nos. 70049-54) were based at Polmadie during their early career, then at Leeds (Holbeck) and elsewhere.

[Brian Morrison]

WR-allocated No. 70026 *Polar Star* was involved in the worst accident with a 'Britannia', in 1955, after three years
service working out of Cardiff (Canton). She was derailed at speed with an up excursion from South Wales on a facing
crossover near Didcot due to the driver not observing a 10 m.p.h. speed restriction; eleven persons were killed and over
150 injured in this derailment. No. 70026 came to rest on soft ground down an embankment and, after overhaul, was
soon back in service. She is seen here outside Canton depot in July 1957, showing the revised arrangement of inset
handholds on the smoke deflectors introduced on WR and other 'Britannias' after this 1955 accident to improve the
driver's forward view.   [Brian Morrison]

No. 70017 *Arrow*, first of the WR 'Britannias', waiting to leave Birmingham (Snow Hill) on 9
March 1958, with the 5.15 p.m. to Cardiff. She exhibits another revised arrangement of handholds
and short grab rails differing from those on No. 70026 opposite.   [M. Mensing]

The latter part of the 'Britannias' main period of service was in the era of indifferent maintenance and almost non-existent cleaning. Little of the unlined green 'economy' livery shows through the accumulated coat of filth and grime on the driver's side of No. 70027 *Rising Star* on shed at Crewe (South) depot, in April 1967. Plainly visible on this side is the live steam injector and the suspension of the rear trailing truck.

[N. E. Preedy]

The fireman's side of No. 70038 *Robin Hood* at York in July 1967, in rather better fettle than No. 70027, smartened up for an enthusiasts' rail tour. The cab of the 'Britannias' was similar to the 9Fs, with extended rigid floor cantilevered out from the boiler over the tender, without any fall-plate. At speed, a considerable backdraught was generated in the gap here, giving rise to a draughty and noisy cab as well as a great deal of swirling coal dust. To minimise this, rubber bellows were fitted, as seen on No. 70038. Otherwise the cabs were commodious and well-laid out, although the 'Britannias' were never pleasant to ride.

[N. E. Preedy]

Two of the 1953-built 'Britannias' were turned out with Westinghouse airbrakes as part of a programme of brake trials held on LM Region in the mid-1950s. With compressors prominent alongside the smokebox and no deflectors, Nos. 70043 and 70044 looked radically different from the rest of the class; both were stationed at Longsight shed (Manchester) and used on the Midland main line on freight train trials as well as normal passenger working. No. 70044, at Longsight on 24 August 1955, was then not named but was christened later. Both locomotives had this airbrake equipment removed subsequently and smoke deflectors added.

[Brian Morrison]

No. 70050 *Firth of Clyde* at Crewe (North) with the later Class 1D tender, provided with the final ten engines (Nos. 70045-54). These had curved self-trimming sides and steam-operated coal pusher, carrying 9 tons of coal instead of the usual BR1 type of 7 ton capacity. All-up weight of a 'Britannia' with the former was 148 tons 10 cwt. compared with 141 tons 4 cwt. with the smaller tender.

[J. R. Carter]

No. 70000 *Britannia* outside Crewe works following general overhaul in the early 1960s.   [E. N. Kneale]

The front end profile of No. 70006 *Robert Burns* at Kingmoor shed, Carlisle, on 6 September 1964. From 1961 onwards most of the WR 'Britannias', plus various ER ones, were transferred to LM Region, many of them to Kingmoor, Upperby or Canal sheds at Carlisle.

[R. H. Leslie]

No. 70041 *Sir John Moore*, in work-a-day condition, at speed near Sandy in Bedfordshire on 7 August 1961 with the 4.12 p.m. Kings Cross to Cleethorpes. An early problem which occurred with 'Britannias' was a fore-and-aft surging movement imparted to the coaches nearest to the tender at about 60 m.p.h. under certain conditions of running. This was cured by altering the tender drawbar spring.

[M. Mensing]

'Britannias' (Nos. 70030-33) had been tried at Holyhead (and Edge Hill shed) late in 1952—following brief early trials in North Wales a year or so before—where they were well liked by the men, but their 7-ton tender capacity was found to be insufficient and they had to be sent on elsewhere—in this case to Longsight shed at Manchester. The last ten 'Britannias' with their 9-ton capacity tenders enabled a further allocation to be made to the North Wales terminus again, where they settled down on 'The Irish Mail' and other expresses, working turn and turn about with rebuilt 'Royal Scots.' Here No. 70045 *Lord Rowallan* pauses at Rugby with the up 'Irish Mail' in July 1959. This locomotive entered service in June 1954 and ran un-named until 1957, when it was named after the Chief Scout in a ceremony at Euston on 16 July. Late in its career, following some front end damage after a minor collision in 1966, No. 70045 emerged from works with LMSR-style oval-headed buffers in place of the standard round-head type. [M. Jackson]

A Sunday lay-over for No. 70041 *Sir John Moore*, outside Stratford shed in April 1955. This was one of three 'Britannias' later moved to March depot, to work accelerated Kings Cross–Grimsby and Cleethorpes services. [Brian Morrison]

No. 70010 *Owen Glendower* (at March, in 1961) and, below, No. 70033 *Charles Dickens* (at Trafford Park). In 1966 the nameplates of No. 70010 were exchanged for ones bearing the Welsh version of the same name, *Owain Glyndwr*— as carried also on the still surviving Vale of Rheidol 2-6-2T.   [N. E. Preedy collection]

No. 70052 *Firth of Tay*, seen here south of Carlisle in September 1957 with a Glasgow and Edinburgh-Liverpool express, was perhaps the luckiest of the 'Britannias'. In a snowstorm in January 1960, working an overnight express south over Ais Gill summit, she suffered a serious breakage in the offside motion (initiated by slidebars working loose), with the piston rod eventually parting company from the connecting rod, which ultimately lanced into the road-bed. Mercifully the driver had warning as the trouble developed and was running at reduced speed but nevertheless a really major accident was averted only by sheer good fortune—a derailment on one of the high S & C viaducts being one particularly dangerous possibility. As it was, an oncoming Leeds-Carlisle freight was derailed due to damage caused to the down line near Settle and five persons were killed in the leading sleeping coaches of the express.

[R. H. Leslie]

A thirteen-coach load for No. 70051 *Firth of Forth* on the 1 in 200 past Quintinshill signal box north of Gretna Junction, 24 May 1959. A 2-6-4 tank will act as banker on the climb of Beattock ahead.

[R. H. Leslie]

Seen coasting quietly towards Carlisle over the bridge across the River Eden on the up goods line, No. 70023 *Venus* was originally WR-based but ended her days at Kingmoor. Her nameplates by this date, 17 June 1967, had been removed with a view to sale. Both the crew are watching, somewhat anxiously, the working of the exhaust injector in front of the trailing truck.   [N. E. Preedy]

Going well on the approach to Southwaite, between Carlisle and Penrith, on 29 August 1964—No. 70038 *Robin Hood* on a southbound express. Class 7 locomotives on Full Load timings were cleared to take 465 tons from Carnforth to Shap Summit and 550 tons from there to Carlisle, or 330 tons and 450 tons respectively on Special Limit loading. Up trains, from Carlisle to the summit, headed by a Class 7, were allowed 550 tons or 450 tons on these same two loadings.   [R. H. Leslie]

No. 70032 *Tennyson* leaving Rugby with a Manchester-Euston express, 21 May 1955.   [T. E. Williams]

No. 70050 *Firth of Clyde*, from Polmadie, waiting to leave Glasgow (Central) with the 4.30 p.m. to Liverpool and Manchester on 27 May 1961.   [M. Mensing]

No. 70042 *Lord Roberts* moving off from New Street station, Birmingham, with the empty stock of the 8.20 a.m. ex-Carlisle (and Workington) which it had earlier worked down from the north, 23 June 1962.   [M. Mensing]

No. 70031 *Byron* with the 10.20 a.m. Euston to Manchester (via Stoke) approaching Prestbury, north of Macclesfield, on Good Friday, 27 March 1959. It is interesting to note that according to one report in December 1966, No. 70031 was then running with a new red 'plastic' nameplate *Lord Byron*.   [M. Mensing]

One of the two 'Britannias' which at one stage had air brakes fitted, No. 70044 (*Earl Haig*) lays a smoke trail along the four-track main line near Leyland, south of Preston, with an up train of milk tanks from Carlisle, July 1965.   [K. R. Pirt]

No. 70042 *Lord Roberts*, again, with the 8.23 a.m. Workington–Euston train on Sunday 25 June 1961. She is approaching Beechwood Tunnel on the Birmingham–Coventry main line, having been diverted because of engineering works on the Trent Valley route.

[M. Mensing]

Overleaf: No. 70001 *Lord Hurcomb* was an unusual visitor to Kings Norton on 14 April 1963, probably because extra Easter holiday traffic at this date had necessitated using the 'Midland' carriage sidings there for some 'North-Western' traffic; No. 70001, now on LM Region and stationed at Willesden, makes a slow start for Birmingham (New Street) with a train of empty stock.

[P. J. Shoesmith]

No. 70022 *Tornado* with a Manchester express passing the site of former Monument Lane station about a mile out of Birmingham (New Street) on 19 April 1963. [P. J. Shoesmith]

No. 70046 *Anzac*, built in June 1954 and running without a name until September 1959, had lost her nameplates by July 1966 when she was photographed 'under the wires' at Crewe. Her high-sided BR1D Class tender is plainly seen, with steam escaping from the coal-pusher.

[E. N. Kneale]

On the Midland main line out of St. Pancras, the 'Britannias' were well thought of, and eight of the class (later ten) were in use out of Trafford Park shed up to 1961—when they were transferred to Willesden for Western Division use on parcels trains and express freights; No. 70052 *Firth of Tay* at St. Pancras on a special in 1965.   [L. Waters]

No. 70000 *Britannia* with an up express for Euston on 3 May 1964 eases past a p.w. slack near Arley Colliery sidings on the ex-MR Birmingham-Nuneaton line, diverted due to electrification work on the West Coast main line. '*Britannia*', here with a 5A shedplate, ended her active service days in 1966, working out of Newton Heath.   [M. Mensing]
—60b—

No. 70016 *Ariel* at Springs Branch, Wigan, in August 1964. For a time in 1951, when new, she was allocated to Leeds (Holbeck).   [J. R. Carter]   61

No. 70052 *Firth of Tay* again, piloted by a Stanier 2-6-4 tank, heads a Manchester–Glasgow express through Salford on a June morning in 1962. The larger BR1D tender was far better suited to the operational requirements of LM Region, with its longer daily runs on average than the others operating 'Britannias' where the smaller inset 7-ton tender provided sufficient fuel capacity.

[J. R. Carter]

Ex-WR-based No. 70018, transferred to Crewe, emerges from one of the tunnels near Chester (General) with a train of empty stock from Llandudno in September 1964. Her name, *Flying Dutchman*, perpetuated that of a famous GWR locomotive.

[J. R. Carter]

Overleaf: An unflattering but impressive low-level photograph of a 'Britannia'—No. 70038 *Robin Hood*, in July 1967. She was withdrawn the following month after just over 14 years of service. In the foreground is the exhaust steam injector, on the side of the ashpan, and its prominent pipework.

[N. E. Preedy]

The six handholes on the deflectors betrayed the WR members of the class after their modification following the *Polar Star* accident in 1955; No. 70019 *Lightning* crossing the Eden bridge at Carlisle with the 5.30 p.m. Perth parcels, 22 April 1962.
[R. H. Leslie]

Polmadie shed normally turned their engines out in fair condition, but not so No. 70051 *Firth Forth* on 1 October 1961, grimy and unkempt and lacking a cylinder front cover, seen on the clir south from Carlisle.
[R. H. Les]

Much maligned they might have been in some quarters, but a 'Britannia' in good condition, with a hard driver and
fireman used to a shallow fire, could give a good account of itself; No. 70054 *Dornoch Firth*, still in mint condition aft
only a few months of service, comes up the gradient south of Lowgill station in October 1955, with 14-on.

[Brian A. Bu

A clear exhaust and steam to spare for No. 70024, ex-*Vulcan*, leaving Settle with a Carlisle-Leeds parcel train in June 1967. After
some hard work on the long climb to Ais Gill, the fireman has an easy task on the downhill run and can leave the fire to itself.

[K. R. Pirt]

The Carlisle 'Britannias' enjoyed outings on the Waverley Route from time to time, as a change from their more usual duties on the West Coast main line; here, No. 70018 *Flying Dutchman*, transferred north, is near Scotch Dyke with an easily managed four-coach local. [R. H. Leslie]

Far removed from her original shed at Laira when new, and now nearing compulsory retirement, No. 70024 taking water on Tebay troughs with a southbound fitted freight, 10 June 1967. Running fast downhill, with the train 'leaning' on the tender, 'Britannias' were not the most comfortable machines to ride on, rolling, surging and bucking slightly all the while.

[R. H. Leslie]

The two-cylinder 'Britannias' had a sharp staccato exhaust when working hard which, once heard, was pleasantl distinctive; No. 70038 *Robin Hood* raising the echoes near Thrimby Grange box on the climb towards Shap, 22 Jul 1967. During this final summer of steam, the 'Britannias' saw considerable service on excursion and other traffic in th North-West.

[R. H. Lesli

No. 70052 *Firth of Tay* on the 1 in 131 up from Carlisle to Wreay with a Glasgow–Manchester and Liverpool express on 4 June 1961. For several years this was a regular Britannia duty; although it was regarded as something of a 'Cinderella' turn, the heavy trains worked were still fairly demanding. The Manchester portion, divided or combined at Preston, was usually only four or five coaches but with the main Liverpool portion added the load might easily be 14 bogies, and doubleheading was not infrequent due to over-loading.

[R. H. Leslie]

The five members of the class allocated to Holyhead in 1954 were dispersed from there, to Crewe and Chester depots, late in 1959 when the first Class 40s appeared on North Wales expresses, but the 'Britannias' continued to appear on subsidiary workings to the area. Here No. 70051 *Firth of Forth* has just come to a stand by Bangor No. 1 signal box with the Holyhead parcels—a train known to railwaymen by the old name of the 'Horse and Carriage'. The signalman has come down from his box to have the extremely lengthy train drawn forward to clear the crossover at the down end of the platform. Opposite, No. 70051 waiting to leave with the same train.

[E. N. Kneale]

The 'Britannia' design was basically intended to be for mixed-traffic use but it was not until their later years of service that they were seen much on freight working. No. 70011, re-named *Hotspur* in chalk after the removal of her nameplates, saunters through Lancaster with a partly-fitted freight for Preston in July 1967. By this date about half the class had been withdrawn from service.

[N. E. Preedy]

Another 'Britannia'-hauled freight, on the north side of Shap—No. 70012 (ex-*John of Gaunt*) near Calthwaite with a train of empty wagons from Carlisle, 15 April 1967. The braking capability of a 'Britannia' was somewhat suspect for the working of loose-coupled freights and they were rarely seen on such turns.

[R. H. Leslie]

Iron Duke still looked every inch a thoroughbred even in her last few months, re-tendered and de-named, and working a lowly pick-up freight. Her days on the prestige 'Golden Arrow' through the orchards of Kent seem a long remove from the scene here, by Ribblehead sidings on the bleak Settle & Carlisle in June 1967. At this date, her name was painted on the smoke deflectors—neatly, in white on a blue background.   [K. R. Pirt]

Another Kingmoor 'Britannia', near Grayrigg and the entrance to the Lune valley with a returning Blackpool-Glasgow excursion. No. 70032 *Tennyson*, with only a month or two of active service left, has acquired by this date a 9-ton tender from one of the earlier withdrawals.   [D. M. Cox]

Scenes showing No. 70053 (ex-*Moray Firth*) on shed at Banbury, 10 December 1965. Then based on Rugby, she was shortly afterwards transferred to Kingmoor, in the final concentration there of the class. Nos. 70050-54—the Scottish Region 'Britannias'—reverted to roller bearings on all coupled wheels, as with the first 35 of the class, the series in between having plain bearings on the axleboxes of either the driving or other coupled wheels. 'Britannias' were used on the ex-GC main line during this period, the Newton Heath allocation being moved to Neasden and Leicester for this early in 1962. Following withdrawal of services on the GC route later, they were transferred to the North-West.

[D. M. Cox]

An after-dark view of No. 70004 (ex-*William Shakespeare*) outside Patricroft shed in September 1964. Early removal of the nameplates, long before 'Britannias' were due for scrapping, was due to the prevalence of theft of them at a time when their value as collectors' items was rapidly increasing. From their position, bolted on the smoke deflectors, 'Britannia' nameplates were particularly prone to rapid unauthorised disappearance. [J. R. Carter]

By the end of 1964, the Class 7 'Britannias' were the principal express steam locomotives left in service on LM Region—indeed only eight rebuilt 'Scots' or 'Patriots' remained, as well as the last 48 of the 'Jubilees'. No. 70029 (ex-*Shooting Star*) and No. 70012 (ex-*John of Gaunt*) are here seen over the pits outside Crewe South shed in the summer of that year. Being of two-cylinder design and relatively recent construction, they were to outlast the ex-LMS three-cylinder locomotives which had, after all, not been designed to withstand the operating conditions that became the norm in the twilight of steam.

[E. N. Kneale]

Many of the last 'Britannias', with the original 7-ton tenders with inset coal bunker, exchanged these for the bigger 9-ton type when these became spare from later withdrawals. No. 70024, (ex-*Vulcan*) having her tender water supply amply replenished at Carnforth in July 1962, shows the BR1 type, with 4,250 gallon capacity, fitted to the first 25 'Britannias'. The next 25 had 5,000 gallon tenders (BR1A), which were outwardly similar in appearance.   [D. M. Cox]

Carlisle (Kingmoor) was the last refuge of the 'Britannias', all except six finding a home there at one time or another in their final years in 1966-67. Apart from the Southern's Bulleid machines these were then the only Pacifics left in BR service. Derek Cross, in his admirable volume, *BR Standard Steam in Action* writes of the Carlisle footplatemen's preference for the smaller but sturdier Stanier Class 5s which formed Kingmoor's other staple at this time. Here No. 70042 (ex-*Lord Roberts*) has the fire dropped over the ash pits on 29 April 1967, only a few days before withdrawal.

[D. M. Cox]

Nos. 70042 and 70012 at Kingmoor, 29 April 1967. The majority of the class had come to be fitted with modified smoke deflectors without handrails, but not the latter. She has also had the automatic warning system removed. In January 1967, 42 'Britannias' remained and further ones were gradually withdrawn through the year, thirteen surviving to the final December deadline. Kingmoor shed at Carlisle was the final outpost of the last 'Britannias', the class being moved there in successive batches as they became redundant at the various depots on other regions following the spread of dieselisation. Kingmoor was also one of the last sheds on BR to operate steam (closed on New Year's Day 1968 and replaced by a new diesel depot); even in June 1967 as many as a hundred locomotives might be seen there at one time, with perhaps half of these in steam and twenty of them 'Britannias' still in running order.

[D. M. Cox]

No. 70013 *Oliver Cromwell*, on the traverser outside Crewe works early in 1967, after general overhaul with a view to preservation. The original intention of BR was to preserve No. 70000 and this had officially been made known as early as 1961 but the latter was in such poor condition by the end of 1966, after a period in open store at Stratford—where vandalism by local youths was rife—that No. 70013 was substituted instead, as an example of the class for preservation. She was the last steam locomotive to be overhauled at Crewe works for BR use, and a minor ceremony marked the occasion when she was outshopped on 2 February.

[E. N. Kneale]

Overleaf: No. 70013 was given special employment for several months after the withdrawal of the rest of the class, hauling various enthusiasts' specials in the North-West. Here, at Blackburn on 28 July 1968, in running condition comparable to her early days in East Anglia, the sight and sound of BR's last operational express steam locomotive arouses the usual scenes of enthusiastic fervour.

[Norman E. Preedy]

No. 70013 *Oliver Cromwell* passing Kirkham with a football excursion returning from Carlisle to Blackpool on Boxing Day 1967. In the last two years or so of the class, they roamed far and wide on a considerable variety of duties, some of which took them to localities hitherto seldom if ever visited by 7P Pacifics. They were frequently seen on freights and parcels trains working into Aberdeen, helping work the Newhaven-Stirling car sleeper at the latter point, on freights at Ellesmere Port, on boat trains to Stranraer, and one even wandered on to the Southern in May 1966, heading Southampton boat trains for a time. And as substitutes for failed diesels, they might turn up anywhere from the Midlands to Aberdeen on passenger trains.

[K. R. Pirt]

No. 70026 *Polar Star* undergoing a mileage overhaul in the running shed at Llandudno Junction in the early 1960s. Dirty and badly worn valves due to excessive carbonisation were one of the features requiring most attention on 'Britannias', although by and large they ran mileages between shoppings comparable to other Class 7 locomotives, despite the declining maintenance standards experienced by steam units when once the new diesels had come into widespread service.

[E. N. Kneale]

End of the road for former No. 70023 *Venus*, inside Newton Heath shed at Manchester on 20 April 1968. Condemned at the end of 1967, she has been stripped of her motion ready for the last run to the breaker's yard.   [P. J. Shoesmith]

No. 70013 in Crewe works undergoing her major overhaul, 15 January 1967. By this date, steam locomotive repair here was relegated to a single road in the machine shop, so as not to interfere with the main business of diesels.

[N. E. Preedy]

No. 70014 was not so lucky as her No. 70013 'sister', for she was to be scrapped in 1968. *Iron Duke* had a more varied career than most of the class, serving at a wide variety of sheds including Norwich, Stewarts Lane, Trafford Park, Newton Heath, Carlisle, Upperby and, finally, Carlisle Kingmoor. This view is at Upperby, in April 1965, when she was still in good mechanical condition—as she is said to have remained to the end. Sold for scrap early in 1968, she languished in store at Carstairs for a brief time and was then towed to a shipbreaker's yard at Inverkeithing to be broken up. With her at the same time went No. 70035 *Rudyard Kipling*, the majority of 'Britannias' being scrapped in this part of Scotland.

[D. M. Cox]

No. 70013 and a Class 5 (No. 45110, also due for preservation) doubleheading an enthusiasts' special at Entwhistle, between Blackburn and Bolton, on 17 March 1968. [D. M. Cox]
Below, making her final run in BR service, No. 70013 running light near Ais Gill, returning south after working the final BR steam special over the section from Manchester to Carlisle, 11 August 1968. [V. C. K. Allen]

After working the special over the Settle & Carlisle, as mentioned overleaf, No. 70013 was serviced at Lostock Hall and then ran back via Blackburn and Todmorden to Doncaster, continuing south the following day (12 August), light engine, to a permanent retirement home at Bressingham Gardens in Norfolk. This, appropriately enough, is in the heart of East Anglia, where the first of the 'Britannias', including No. 70013, first saw service. Here, she is seen in steam again, immaculate and with her 32a shedplate restored, amid the setting Alan Bloom has provided for a truly magnificent collection of former main line steam.   [S. Creer]

acknowledgments: the editor and publishers wish to thank the many photographers whose work appears in this volume and without whom it could not have been compiled.

MIDLAND
OF THE BORDER
NORTH EASTERN
STEAM
GREAT WESTERN
STEAM MISCELLANY
STEAM
BODMIN AND WADEBRIDGE
FROM LINES
GREAT WESTERN
BR STANDARD STEAM
BRITISH
NARROW GAUGE
STEAM
A PICTORIAL SURVEY
BRANCH LINE STEAM
DIESELS
ON SCOTTISH REGION
BR DIESELS
IN THE LANDSCA
IN ACTION
BR DIESELS
BRITISH
H. C. CASSERLEY
IRISH RAILWAYS
in the heyday of steam
OPEAN
EAM
ERN
MOTIVE
SOUTHERN 188
RAILWA
IN ACTION
THE WARSHIPS
THE LYNTON & BARNSTAPLE RAILWAY
THE WAINWRIGHT
ASSES
STEAM
NORTH EASTERN
STEAM
N ACTION
LONDON MIDLAND
STEAM IN ACTION 4
42/43 DIESEL - HYDRAULICS
LONDON
RT
BUS
SOUTHERN
8F
8-0
GREAT
CENTRAL
recalled